EYE to EYE with ANIMALS

CARNIVOROUS BIG CATS

by Ruth Owen

WINDMILL
BOOKS

Published in 2013 by Windmill Books, An Imprint of Rosen Publishing
29 East 21st Street, New York, NY 10010

Produced for Windmill by Ruby Tuesday Books Ltd
Editor for Ruby Tuesday Books Ltd: Mark J. Sachner
US Editor: Sara Antill
Designer: Emma Randall

Photo Credits:
Cover, 1, 4–5, 7, 8–9, 11, 12–13, 15, 16–17, 19, 20–21, 23, 24–25, 27, 28–29 ©
Shutterstock.

Library of Congress Cataloging-in-Publication Data

Owen, Ruth, 1967–
 Carnivorous big cats / by Ruth Owen.
     p. cm. — (Eye to eye with animals)
 Includes index.
 ISBN 978-1-4488-8069-0 (library binding) — ISBN 978-1-4488-8105-5 (pbk.) —
ISBN 978-1-4488-8111-6 (6-pack)
 1. Felidae—Juvenile literature. I. Title.
 QL737.C23O937 2013
 599.75—dc23

                                        2012009788

Manufactured in the United States of America

CPSIA Compliance Information: Batch # B2S12WM: For Further Information contact Windmill Books, New York, New York at 1-866-478-0556

CONTENTS

Meet the Big Cats!

They have sharp teeth, huge paws, and powerful bodies, and they are very skillful hunters. Meet the big cats!

The world's big cats are the large, wild relatives of the small, fluffy creatures that share our homes. There are 38 different **species**, or types, of cats. They are all **carnivores**, or meat eaters, that use their senses, speed, or strength to catch their **prey**. Big cats live in many different **habitats**, from **grasslands** to jungles, mountains, and **swamps**.

Sadly, humans have not respected or been kind to the world's wild cats and many are now **endangered**. In this book, you can go eye-to-eye with some of the world's biggest and most beautiful hunters, and find out what the future holds for them.

An African lioness and cubs

4

BIG CATS IN DANGER

Big cats face a difficult future. The places where they live are being destroyed. They are hunted by humans for their fur, or for their body parts, which are used in **traditional** medicines. Some types of big cats have actually been hunted to **extinction**!

TIGERS
The Biggest Big Cats

Length including tail: 6.5 to 12 feet (1.9–3.7 m)

Weight: 200 to 930 pounds (91–420 kg)

Weight at birth: 2.6 pounds (1.2 kg)

Lifespan: 8 to 26 years

Breeding age (females): 3.5 years

Breeding age (males): 5 years

Diet: Prey includes deer, wild pigs, monkeys, birds, and fish

Habitat: Some species of tigers live in hot tropical forests. Others live in snowy evergreen forests.

FACE FACTS

Some of the markings on a tiger's forehead look like the Chinese character *wang*. In English, "wang" means "king". In China it is believed that the tiger is the king of all the animals.

Adult Siberian tiger

Tigers are the largest cats. They hunt alone, attacking large prey, such as deer. Their stripes keep them hidden among trees and plants.

An Expert Hunter

Tigers mainly hunt at night. A tiger will eat around 60 pounds (27 kg) of meat in one meal. When it is full, it hides the **carcass** under leaves and dirt so it can return to its prize later. An adult tiger can drag a dead animal that would take 13 men to move.

Tiger Families

Adult males and females only come together to **mate**. Females give birth to between one and seven cubs in a **litter**. The cubs drink milk from their mother's body for the first six months of their lives. They learn to hunt by watching their mother sneak up on prey. Cubs stay with their mothers for two to three years.

A tiger's back legs are longer than its front legs. This helps it leap distances up to 32 feet (10 m).

THE CAT THAT LOVES WATER!

Tigers are strong swimmers. They have been tracked swimming distances of 20 miles (32 km) without stopping to rest.

Endangered Tigers

Scientists believe there are fewer than **5,000** tigers left on Earth.

This number includes Bengal tigers, Indo-Chinese tigers, Sumatran tigers, and Siberian tigers. The South China tiger is possibly extinct.

The Bali tiger, Caspian tiger, and Javan tiger have been extinct for many years.

Tigers are hunted for their skins and for their body parts that are used in Chinese medicine. Their forest habitat is cut down for lumber or to make space for villages and farms.

TIGERS RANGE MAP

The red areas on the map show where tigers live wild.

This tiger cub is less than a week old.

9

AFRICAN LIONS
Family Guys

Length including tail: Up to 10 feet (3 m)

Weight: 280 to 530 pounds (127–240 kg)

Weight at birth: 3.3 pounds (1.5 kg)

Lifespan: 10 to 15 years

Breeding age (females): 4 years

Breeding age (males): 5 years

Diet: Prey includes zebras, antelope, wildebeest, giraffes, warthogs, and hares

Habitat: Grasslands and wooded areas in Africa

FACE FACTS

Adult male lions grow a thick mane of hair. The mane helps to make a male look large and impressive when fighting other males. The mane also protects the lion's head and neck during fights.

Adult male lion

African lions live in family groups called prides. They are the only species of big cats to live in groups.

Family Life
An adult male lion leads and protects a pride of lionesses and their cubs. He is the father of all the cubs. Female lions stay with their pride for life. A young male leaves his family when he is two to three years old. When he is big and strong enough, he fights an older male and takes over that male's pride.

It's All About Teamwork!
Lions are **predators** that hunt as a team. The lionesses do most of the hunting and they may catch an animal every two to three days. A lioness gives birth to a litter of up to six cubs. Cubs drink milk from their mother, and sometimes from the other females in the pride. The lionesses often babysit for each other's cubs.

A lion pride shares a meal.

ASIATIC LIONS

There are two types of lions—African lions and Asiatic lions. Asiatic lions are critically endangered. They live wild in one place on Earth, a protected park in the Gir Forest, in India.

Endangered Lions

There are just **350 Asiatic lions left in the wild.**

There are only around **25,000 African lions left in the wild.**

Asiatic lions have been hunted almost to extinction.

African lions are losing their grassland habitat, which is being turned into farmland.

In some parts of Africa, hunters are allowed to shoot lions for sport.

Cubs often tease and play with their huge father!

LIONS RANGE MAP

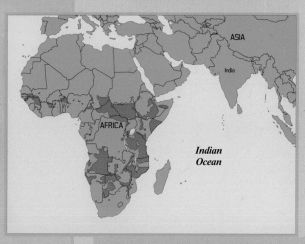

The red areas on the map show where lions live wild.

Cubs have spotted coats to help them hide in long grass from predators, such as leopards.

13

LEOPARDS
The Climbing Big Cats

Length including tail: Up to 10 feet (3 m)

Weight: 37 to 143 pounds (17–65 kg)

Weight at birth: 1 pound (0.5 kg)

Lifespan: 12 to 15 years

Breeding age (females): 2.5 years

Breeding age (males): 2 years

Diet: Prey includes antelope, gazelles, deer, wild pigs, monkeys, and birds

Habitat: Grasslands, forests, mountains, and deserts in Africa and Asia. Leopards prefer areas with trees.

FACE FACTS

Leopards have large heads with powerful jaws. They have long eyebrows that help to protect their eyes when they are moving through thick bushes, grasses, or tree branches.

Adult leopard

15

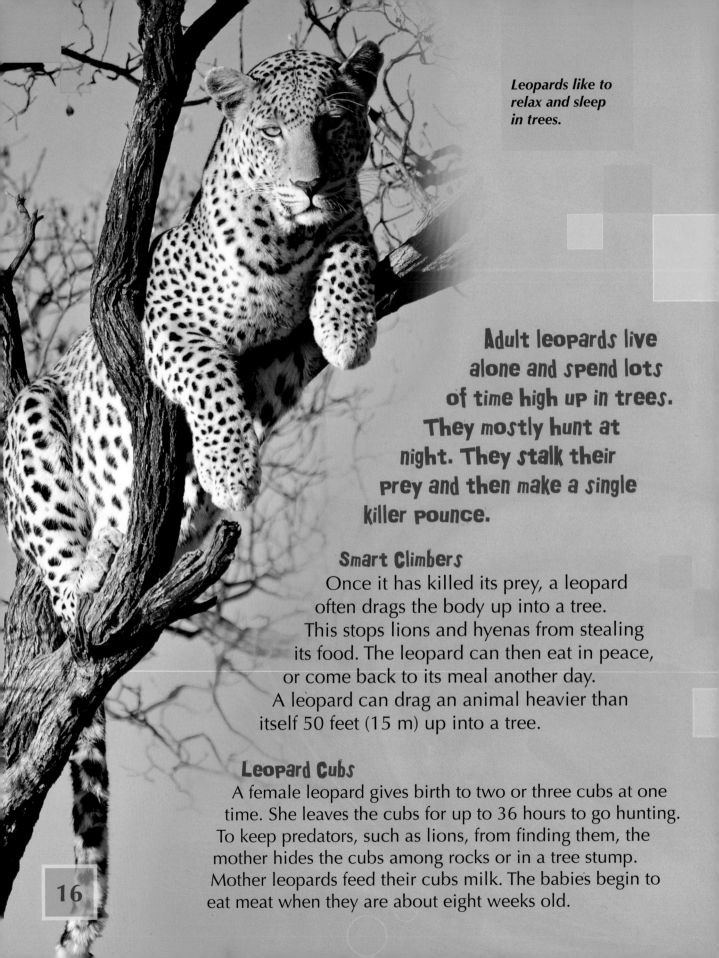

Leopards like to relax and sleep in trees.

Adult leopards live alone and spend lots of time high up in trees. They mostly hunt at night. They stalk their prey and then make a single killer pounce.

Smart Climbers

Once it has killed its prey, a leopard often drags the body up into a tree. This stops lions and hyenas from stealing its food. The leopard can then eat in peace, or come back to its meal another day. A leopard can drag an animal heavier than itself 50 feet (15 m) up into a tree.

Leopard Cubs

A female leopard gives birth to two or three cubs at one time. She leaves the cubs for up to 36 hours to go hunting. To keep predators, such as lions, from finding them, the mother hides the cubs among rocks or in a tree stump. Mother leopards feed their cubs milk. The babies begin to eat meat when they are about eight weeks old.

LEOPARD ATHLETES

Leopards can run in short bursts at 37 miles per hour (60 km/h) and cover 20 feet (6 m) in a single leap. They are also good swimmers.

Leopards have coats covered with black spots and shapes known as rosettes.

Endangered Leopards
Leopards are in danger from hunting and because their forest habitat is disappearing.

Leopards have been hunted by people for many years for their beautiful fur.

Leopards are sometimes killed for their whiskers, which people use in medicines.

Leopards sometimes kill farm animals, so farmers shoot them.

LEOPARD RANGE MAP

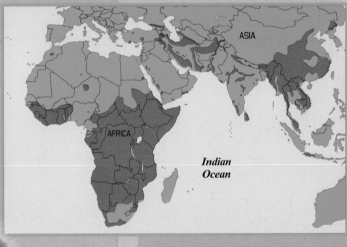

The red areas on the map show where leopards live wild.

A two-month-old leopard cub

CHEETAHS
The Grassland Sprinters

Length including tail: Up to 7.5 feet (2.3 m)

Weight: 86 to 143 pounds (39 to 65 kg)

Weight at birth: 0.6 pound (272 g)

Lifespan: 7 to 14 years

Breeding age (females): 2 years

Breeding age (males): 2 years

Diet: Prey such as antelope, gazelles, young warthogs, porcupines, rabbits, and birds

Habitat: Grasslands in Africa; a small number live in Iran

FACE FACTS

Cheetahs have a black line running down from each eye. Scientists believe these lines make it easier for a cheetah to see in bright sunshine. They cut down on glare from the Sun, a little like cheetah sunglasses.

Cheetahs are the fastest land animals on Earth. An adult cheetah hunts alone, using its speed to catch fast prey.

Fast Food

A cheetah attack usually lasts for less than a minute. Once a cheetah has decided on a victim, it attacks and gives chase. A cheetah can run at up to 70 miles per hour (113 km/h). It covers about 20 feet (6 m) with every stride. If a cheetah makes a kill, it needs to get its breath back for about 20 minutes. Then the cheetah must eat fast before a lion, leopard, or hyena steals its food.

Moms and Cubs

A female cheetah usually gives birth to between three and five cubs. The babies stay with their mother for around 18 months learning how to hunt. Young females then leave their mother and go off alone. Brothers sometimes stay together until they are adults.

A cheetah cub and its mother's tail

A cheetah chasing a warthog

Endangered Cheetahs

About 100 years ago there were 100,000 cheetahs in Africa. Today, there are just 12,000 left.

The cheetah's grassland home is being turned into farmland by people.

Farmers sometimes kill cheetahs to keep them from hunting farm animals.

Cheetahs are daytime hunters. Their daily lives and hunts are sometimes disturbed by tourists on wildlife-watching vacations.

CHEETAH CHAT

Cheetahs cannot roar like lions or tigers. They "talk" to each other using purrs, growls, hisses, coughs, and moans. When they are excited, they make a chirping noise like a bird.

CHEETAH RANGE MAP

The red areas on the map show where cheetahs live wild.

A cheetah family

MOUNTAIN LIONS
The Cat of Many Names

Length including tail: 5 to 8 feet (1.5–2.5 m)

Weight: 80 to 230 pounds (36–104 kg)

Weight at birth: Up to 1 pound (0.5 kg)

Lifespan: 20 years

Breeding age (females): 2.5 years

Breeding age (males): 3 years

Diet: Prey includes moose, elk, deer, caribou, wild pigs, beavers, hares, raccoons, skunks, squirrels, and birds

Habitat: Forests, grasslands, and swamps in North, Central, and South America

FACE FACTS

Mountain lions aren't afraid of catching and eating a prickly porcupine. They happily crunch into this spiky prey and even eat the porcupine's quills!

Adult mountain lion

23

Mountain lions are also known as cougars, pumas, and panthers. This big cat has many names, but it is just one species.

Mountain Lion Neighborhoods

Adult mountain lions live alone. Each animal has its own **territory**, or home range, where it hunts. A territory may be as small as 30 square miles (78 sq km), or as large as 125 square miles (324 sq km). A male mountain lion's large territory may include the smaller home ranges of several females. The big cats stay in touch by leaving messages for each other. To do this, they use their urine and waste and scratch marks on logs.

Mothers and Cubs

Female mountain lions give birth in a den set up in a cave or thick bushes. They give birth to three or four cubs at one time. Cubs stay with their mother for six to 12 months until they are able to hunt their own food.

Mountain lions take shelter in caves and among rocks.

POWERFUL JUMPERS

A mountain lion can jump 20 feet (6 m) up a mountainside. That's as high as jumping onto the roof of a two-story building!

Mountain Lions and Humans

Mountain lions have been shot, trapped, or poisoned because people think they are a danger to farm animals.

People often think that mountain lions will attack them when they are hiking or camping. The truth is that these animals are usually afraid of people and just want to be left alone.

MOUNTAIN LION RANGE MAP

The red areas on the map show where mountain lions live wild.

A four-month-old mountain lion cub

SNOW LEOPARDS
The Ghost Cats

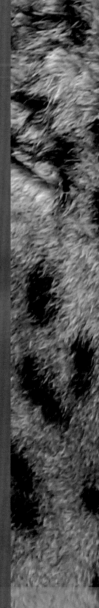

Length including tail: Up to 7.5 feet (2.3 m)

Weight: 55 to 165 pounds (25–75 kg)

Weight at birth: 1 pound (0.5 kg)

Lifespan: Up to 18 years

Breeding age (females): 2 years

Breeding age (males): 2 years

Diet: Prey includes wild sheep, deer, wild boar, marmots, hares, birds, and small mammals, such as mice

Habitat: High up in mountain ranges, cliffs, and evergreen forests in Asia

FACE FACTS

The snow leopard's black markings and smoky-gray fur allow it to blend in with its rocky, mountain habitat.

Adult snow leopard

Snow leopards are shy and live in very steep, cold places. This makes them difficult to spot and study.

Mountain Spirits

If spotted, these big cats soon disappear among rocks. Local people in the countries where they live call them "ghost cats." In **folklore**, they are described as mountain **spirits**.

Snow leopards can jump distances of up to 45 feet (14 m). Their jumping skills allow them to leap from cliff to cliff, or over deep crevices on mountain slopes. They have large paws with fur on the bottom. The fur keeps the leopards from slipping on snow and ice.

Snow Leopard Cubs

Snow leopards are **rare**, and adults live alone. When it's time to breed, males and females find each other by calling out. Females give birth to up to three cubs in a litter. The cubs begin to learn how to hunt at three months old.

WRAPPING UP WARM

Snow leopards have very long tails covered with thick fur. They wrap their tails around their bodies for warmth and cover their faces when the temperature is below freezing.

A snow leopard's tail is nearly as long as its body.

Endangered Snow Leopards

Secretive snow leopards in their high, mountain habitats are hard to study. Scientists know that their numbers are low, but no one knows for sure how many are living wild.

The biggest threat to snow leopards is hunting. They are hunted for their fur. Hunting the cats is against the law, but a coat made from snow leopard fur can be sold for $60,000!

Snow leopard bones are used in traditional Asian medicines even though they have no healing powers!

SNOW LEOPARD RANGE MAP

The red areas on the map show where snow leopards live wild.

A snow leopard cub

GLOSSARY

carcass (KAR-kus)
A dead body, usually of
an animal.

carnivores (KAHR-neh-vorz)
Animals that eat only meat.

endangered (in-DAYN-jerd)
In danger of no longer existing.

extinction (ek-STINGK-shun)
The state of no longer existing.

folklore (FOHK-lohr)
The traditional beliefs and ideas
of a group of people that have
been passed on as stories to the
people who came after them.

grasslands (GRAS-landz)
A hot habitat with lots of
grass and few trees or bushes.
Sometimes it is very dry, and at
other times there is lots of rain.

habitats (HA-buh-tatz)
Places where animals or plants
normally live. A habitat may
be a rain forest, the ocean, or a
backyard.

litter (LIH-ter)
A group of baby animals all
born to the same mother at the
same time.

mate (MAYT)
When a male and female come
together in order to have young.

predators (PREH-duh-terz)
Animals that hunt and kill
other animals for food.

prey (PRAY)
An animal that is hunted by another animal as food.

rare (RER)
Very few in number or in existence.

species (SPEE-sheez)
One type of living thing. The members of a species look alike and can produce young together.

spirits (SPIR-uts)
Ghosts or supernatural forms that are not part of the human world.

stalk (STOK)
To follow without being seen.

swamps (SWOMPS)
Areas of wet, spongy land where plants grow.

territory (TER-uh-tor-ee)
The area where an animal lives, finds its food, and finds partners for mating.

traditional (truh-DIH-shuh-nul)
Something that a group of people have done for many years and have passed on to the people who came after them.

Websites

For web resources related to the subject of this book, go to: www.windmillbooks.com/weblinks and select this book's title.

READ MORE

Jenkins, Martin, and Vicky White. *Can We Save the Tiger?*. Somerville, MA: Candlewick Press, 2011.

Joubert, Beverly, and Dereck Joubert. *Face to Face with Lions*. Face to Face with Animals. Des Moines, IA: National Geographic Children's Books, 2010.

Parker, Steve, and Ian Jackson. *Big Cats*. I Love Animals. New York: Windmill Books, 2011.

Randall, Henry. *Cheetahs*. Cats of the Wild. New York: PowerKids Press, 2011.

INDEX